Countdown to Easter

Lesley Cox and Leslie Foster

Macmillan Education

Contents

1. Countdown to Easter

Nowadays many people think of Christmas as being the best time of the year. It is certainly a happy time which is made exciting by the giving of presents and by the rich food which everybody enjoys. However, the Church believes that Easter is a more important festival than Christmas because at this time Christians remember how Jesus came back to life after being put to death by the Romans.

About a hundred years after the death of Jesus, the first Christians looked on Easter as the greatest of the holy days. Since then Christians all over the world have attended church at Easter to recall the resurrection of Jesus with great happiness and rejoicing.

The Church's Easter season begins early in the calendar year and includes all the festivals from Shrove Tuesday to the eve of Whitsunday. The Church's leaders knew the exact time of the year of the first Easter because it was the date of the Jewish Passover. In AD 325, they met to decide that Easter Day should be on the first Sunday after the full moon, which was on or after the vernal (or spring) equinox. This is the day when the sun is halfway between being nearest to the Earth in midsummer, and farthest from the Earth in midwinter. The equinox is on March 21st, so Easter always falls between March 22nd and April 25th. It is, of course, always in spring.

These are the dates for Easter up to the year 2000:

Year	Date	Year	Date
1985	7 April	1993	11 April
1986	30 March	1994	3 April
1987	19 April	1995	16 April
1988	3 April	1996	7 April
1989	26 March	1997	30 March
1990	15 April	1998	12 April
1991	31 March	1999	4 April
1992	19 April	2000	23 April

Many customs now connected with Easter were celebrated long before Jesus died. Even the name comes from *Eastre* or *Eostre*, who was the goddess of spring, worshipped by pagans before the coming of Christianity. In those days people thought that they had to please the gods, so at the spring equinox they held festivals. In Syria they remembered Adonis, the god of corn, and in Phrygia they honoured the god of plants who was called Attis. The Teutons, who lived at the mouth of the river Elbe, had a festival known as *Eostur*

4

to remember the goddess of spring. The Anglo-Saxons, who lived in Britain about a thousand years ago, called April *Eastur monath*.

In many European countries the words used for Easter are very similar. In France it is *Pâques*, in Spain *Pasena*, in Italy *Pasqua*, in Holland *Paach*, and in Sweden *Påsk*. All these words come from the Hebrew *Pasach* or *Pesakh*, which means 'Passover'. In English we often speak of 'the Paschal lamb' or 'the Paschal candle', meaning that they are to do with Easter.

In spring the whole world of nature comes back to life again after the winter months. People are glad to say goodbye to the cold, dark days and welcome the lighter, longer, warmer days of spring. Many old Easter customs deal with stories of being reborn, and include magic spells to make the crops grow again. The customs connected with hot-cross buns, Easter eggs and the Easter hare go far back into history, but have been given Christian meanings.

The story of the last days in the life of Jesus is both sad and happy. So many things happened that it is not surprising that the writers of the gospels wrote far more about this week than they did about anything else in the life of Jesus. The first Easter was such an important event that it changed the history of the world and gave birth to its greatest religion.

This book tells the story of those times and describes some of the customs connected with the festival. Some activities have been suggested and are to be found at the end of each chapter. They have been arranged in order of difficulty and it is hoped that they will add to the enjoyment of the book as children 'countdown' to Easter.

5

2. Shrovetide

L ife for many people in olden times was so hard that they enjoyed a break from their work on the holy days which we now call holidays. No sooner had the Twelve Days of Christmas festivities ended on January 6th (Epiphany) than they looked forward to the period of merrymaking during the four days before the start of *Lent*. Lent was a time of strictness and going without certain foods, so Shrovetide became a festival of jollification, rough games and eating before the six quiet weeks of Lent began.

The word *shrove* comes from the old word *shrive* which means 'to cleanse' or 'forgive'. It was the custom on the day before Lent started for Christians to go to church to tell the priest what things they had done wrong. When he had heard their confession, and had given them God's forgiveness, they felt themselves shriven, or cleansed of their sins. These few days before Ash Wednesday were called Shrovetide and hence Shrove Tuesday, which was a holiday many years ago. Shrove Tuesday is always six weeks and three days before Easter.

Just as the Jews eat all the unleavened bread before the Passover, so Christians ate all the rich food before the start of Lent. By custom meat, butter and cream were not eaten during this season so, on Shrove Monday, all the meat was used up to make a special dish which was like a pâté made up into a steak. It was called a collop, and the day was known as Collop Monday. Bacon and eggs were also eaten with the fried collops of meat on this day.

The next day it was time to use up all the butter and cream, and this was usually done by making pancakes. In Britain, Shrove Tuesday is more often called 'Pancake Day' and most families make, toss and eat pancakes at some time during the day. It is possible that the origin of pancakes goes back to the Roman Feast of Ovens when small wheat cakes were eaten some time in February. In some parts of England, Shrove Tuesday was known as Guttit Tuesday or Goodish Day because of the good things which were eaten.

On Pancake Day in many parts of Britain, pancake races are run. These races are thought to have started when a housewife who was cooking pancakes heard the church bells ring. Thinking that she was late for the service, she ran off still holding the pan in her hand.

The most famous pancake race is run on Shrove Tuesday at Olney in Buckinghamshire. This race was first mentioned in 1445 and has certainly been run there every year since 1948. Housewives have to live in the

Olney Pancake Race

7

area to be allowed to take part in the competition. A bell rings to tell them to start making their pancakes and it rings again to tell them to go to the starting line with their cooked pancakes in a frying pan. The bell rings a third time to start the race. Wearing aprons, and with their heads covered by a scarf, the women have to run about a quarter of a mile from the village square to the parish church. They have to toss their pancakes three times during the race and are allowed to pick them up if they drop them. The vicar waits at the church door to greet the winner and gives her a prayer book as a prize. The verger or bell-ringer has two rewards: a kiss from the winner, and her pancake. All the frying pans are laid in the church font during the short service which follows the race.

A similar race is run on Shrove Tuesday in the town of Liberal, Kansas, in the United States of America and a competition is now held to see whether Olney or Liberal provides the quicker winner. The races are run in both places and the latest records for the 380 metres (415 yards) course are 61 seconds by Sally Ann Faulkner of Olney on February 26th, 1974 and 58.5 seconds by Sheila Turner of Liberal on February 11th, 1975.

At Westminster School, in London, a custom called the Pancake Greeze is observed on Shrove Tuesday. The school cook enters the Great Schoolroom at eleven o'clock in the morning carrying a pancake in his frying pan. He tosses the pancake over an iron bar, which is 5 metres (16 feet) high, and boys from each form scramble for it. The boy who retrieves the biggest part of the pancake wins the prize of one guinea (£1.05).

Until the eighteenth century Shrove Tuesday was a holiday and was the excuse for letting off steam before the start of the solemn season of Lent. Men and boys

Pancake Greeze, Westminster School

got up to all sorts of pranks, practical jokes and wild games. They engaged in wrestling and horse racing and in cruel practices such as cock-fighting, thrashing hens and throwing stones at cockerels which were fastened to a post. Fortunately these practices are no longer allowed.

Things to do

1   Why do we eat pancakes on Shrove Tuesday? Describe one of the old pancake customs.

2   On a map of England write the places where games are played on Shrove Tuesday. In a box under the place put the name of the game played.

3   How did Shrove Tuesday get its name? What happened in church on this day?

4   Why did people enjoy Shrovetide so much in days gone by? What sort of things did they do at this time?

5   Work out in kilometres or miles per hour, the speed of the winners of the pancake races in Olney, Buckinghamshire and Liberal, Kansas.
Give an estimate first and then work out more exact answers.

6   Try your hand at making some pancakes. It would be a good idea to have the help of an adult while you do this.
You will need:
   lard, or cooking fat, or cooking oil
   110 g (4 oz) flour (plain, if possible)
   2 eggs
   300 ml ($\frac{1}{2}$ pint) milk
   pinch of salt

Sieve the flour and salt into a fairly large basin. Break the eggs and add them to the flour. Add a quarter of the milk and stir with a wooden spoon until the flour is blended. Then beat the mixture hard until it is smooth. Beat in the rest of the milk and then use an egg whisk or rotary whisk to put air into the mixture.

Let the batter stand for a short time in a cool place.

Put about 25–30 ml (1 oz) of fat or oil into a frying pan and heat it until a faint haze appears. Pour the batter from a jug to cover the pan thinly and cook steadily on one side for about two minutes. Toss the pancake: shake the pan, insert a broad-bladed knife or slice under the pancake and give it a gentle turn.

Cook for another two minutes on the other side and then remove the pancake on to a warm dish. Flavour the pancake with sugar and lemon juice.

Heat some more fat in the pan and cook the next pancake.

3. Ash Wednesday and Lent

Ash Wednesday is the day after Shrove Tuesday and is the time when many Christians attend church. In Roman Catholic and many Anglican churches the priest blesses the ashes from the previous year's burned palms. He then makes a cross with the ash on the foreheads of the congregation and says the words, 'Remember man that thou art dust and unto dust shalt thou return.' This act recalls the many times that people in the Old Testament stories used to put ashes on their heads as a sign of sorrow or to ask forgiveness for their sins.

Ash Wednesday is the first day of Lent, when some Christians begin a solemn period as they remember how Jesus went into a wild part of the desert to prepare for his future work of preaching and teaching. During those forty days we are told that Jesus went without food and spent his time in prayer. Also, he had to decide how to make ordinary people understand what he was saying. They would listen to him if he did magic tricks such as turning stones into bread or throwing himself off the top of the Temple without getting hurt. There were several ways of becoming so well-known that he would soon have had a great following. But he decided against these methods and left the wilderness to begin three years' work as an ordinary teacher.

The word Lent comes from the old English *Lencten*, which means 'spring' or 'springtime'. Lent lasts for exactly forty days from Ash Wednesday to Easter

Sunday, if the Sundays during that period are excluded. Just as Jesus spent the time in the wilderness fasting and praying, so many Christians eat less during Lent and spend more time praying and reading special religious books. It is an important time for Christian Churches, and Roman Catholics hold a special mass every day in Lent. Some people give up special food such as chocolates or sweets. They cut down on their amusements and give the money they save to good causes such as Missions to other countries. Many churches do not have weddings during this time and do not decorate their buildings with flowers.

The season began many years ago to remind people to prepare themselves for Easter by remembering the way Jesus suffered and died. Some Christians compare it to a bride (the Church) mourning for the death of her bridegroom (Jesus Christ). The length of Lent has changed over the years. At one time the period of fasting was thirty-six days but, during the reign of Charlemagne in AD 800, four days were added to make it as long as the forty days Jesus spent in the desert.

The fourth Sunday in Lent has various names including *Refreshment Sunday*, *Mid-Lent Sunday*, *Simnel Sunday* and *Mothering Sunday*. It is the proper day for eating simnel cakes. These cakes vary in shape and contents but the most popular ones have a hard crust of almond pastry and are decorated with candied fruits and marzipan. Many cakes are still sent abroad in time to be eaten on Simnel Sunday. It is not known for sure how the cake got its name, but it probably came from the Latin word for the fine wheat flour from which the cakes are made.

The day is best known as 'Mothering Sunday'. This name came from the habit, which started more than

three hundred years ago, of going to the Mother-church in the parish to give money on this day. Since that time families have gathered together on Mothering Sunday and children, who had left home, returned to bring gifts to their mothers. It appears that apprentices and servants were given a holiday on this day to visit their mothers and take with them a simnel cake, violets or other spring flowers they had picked on the way. Sometimes the whole family went to church and returned home afterwards to a special dinner of roast lamb, rice pudding, ale and home-made wine.

'On Mothering Day above all other
Every child should dine with its mother.'

The old custom took on a new look when the American servicemen were stationed in the British Isles during the Second World War. Our old 'Mothering Day' customs and their own 'Mothers' Day', which was started in 1907 and is held in the United States on the second Sunday in May, became confused. So now the two occasions are held on the same day, although they have quite different histories. Nowadays absent sons and daughters usually send their mothers a card or present and children at home give a card, flowers or some other gift. Shopkeepers and florists take advantage of this and flowers are especially expensive at this time.

Things to do

1 Make a Mothers' Day card. The design on the front may have spring flowers on it. The message or verse inside will say how you feel about your mother on this special day.

2 Read the passages from the Gospels in the New Testament which tell the story of the time Jesus spent in the wilderness. You will find them in:
  St. Matthew: Chapter 4, verses 1 to 11;
  St. Mark: Chapter 1, verses 12 and 13;
  St. Luke: Chapter 4, verses 1 to 13.

3 Write your own account of what happened to Jesus during his forty days in the desert.

4 Who was Charlemagne? When did he live and why is he famous?

5 Ask an adult to make a simnel cake with you. You will find the recipe in any good cookery book. To decorate the cake you can use real or artificial primroses. These can be made with left-over marzipan. A large bow of yellow ribbon will make the cake look most attractive.

6 What could you give up during Lent? It must be something you enjoy otherwise you will not miss it. Perhaps you and your classmates could give the money you have saved to a favourite charity.

7 Make a graph to show what members of your class will miss most; for example, sweets, biscuits, cakes, chocolate.

14

4. Passion Sunday and Palm Sunday

The fifth Sunday in Lent is known as *Passion Sunday* and the term comes from the Latin word which means 'suffering'. The sufferings of Jesus towards the end of his life are often referred to as his 'passion', and plays written to represent the trial and death of Jesus are known as *Passion plays*.

The most famous of these is the one produced at Oberammergau in Germany and its origin goes back three hundred and fifty years. A plague had been

Oberammergau Passion Play

raging in the neighbourhood and, when it was over, the villagers made a vow that they would give thanks for deliverance by putting on a play every ten years. They have kept their promise ever since that time, with two exceptions: once after the First World War and again in 1940. The actors spend much time rehearsing the play and twelve hundred people take part in the performance. The play lasts for eight hours and attracts visitors from all over the world. The scenes describe realistically the events of the last week of Jesus' Life.

The sixth Sunday in Lent, the one before Easter, is commonly called Palm Sunday. It recalls the journey of Jesus and his disciples to Jerusalem the week before he was put to death. He had wanted to visit the holy city for the great Jewish feast of the Passover. This is the anniversary of the time when Jews believe that the angel of death passed over the houses of the Israelites in Egypt but killed the first-born of the Egyptians. As a result the Hebrews were able to escape from slavery in Egypt and flee to their freedom in the Promised Land.

Jesus had made preparations to spend the Passover, which is also called the Feast of Unleavened Bread, in a certain house and had instructed his disciples to find a donkey which he then rode into Jerusalem. As he entered the city his disciples threw their clothing on the ground for the donkey to walk on.

The Jews were expecting a king who would overthrow their Roman overlords and, when they heard that Jesus was coming, they thought that this was the person who would lead them into battle. They became very excited, tore branches from the palm trees, and met Jesus shouting, 'Here is the man who comes in the name of the Lord! God bless the King of Israel!' Although Jesus had made a joyful entry into Jerusalem, it was not a

moment of triumph for him. He knew that the people were wanting a ruler and not someone who had come to teach them how to lead better lives.

These, and other events, are the ones Christians remember on Palm Sunday. The journey was first celebrated sixteen hundred years ago by the Christian Church in Jerusalem when a procession set off from the Mount of Olives. A bishop played the part of Jesus and rode on a donkey into the city as children sang and waved branches. Since that day processions have been held in churches, and priests have read the story of the trial and crucifixion of Jesus. Very often branches of laurel, olive and willow trees were used on Palm Sunday instead of palms. Nowadays, children and members of the congregation are given a cross made of palm leaves in church on this day.

At one time in Great Britain, people used to go 'a-palming' on the two or three days before Palm Sunday. There are, of course, few real palm trees in

Britain, but folk used to go into the woods to collect green branches to hang in their houses and churches. They also cut sprigs of green twigs to put in their hats and pin on their coats. People also gathered twigs of hazel, willow and yew. In many parts of the country the willow is still called the English Palm and it was believed that if it was gathered for the festival, and taken home, the house would be protected from evil.

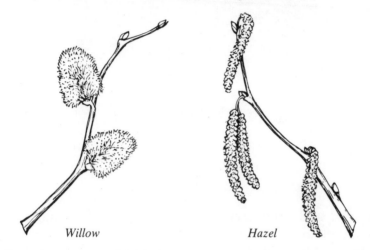

Willow   Hazel

In some parts of Britain, and especially in Wales, the day is called 'Flowering Sunday'. This arose from the custom of visiting churchyards on Palm Sunday to tidy the graves ready for Easter. Friends and relatives used to weed the ground, whitewash the stones and put spring flowers and evergreens on the graves of loved ones.

Things to do

1   Read the poem by G. K. Chesterton called 'The Donkey'. Write the events of the first Palm Sunday as described by the donkey. All donkeys have a raised cross shape on their backs, and legend has it that the donkey was given the cross in memory of Palm Sunday.

2   Read the story of the ride into Jerusalem from a modern version of the Bible. These passages will interest you:

St. Matthew: Chapter 26, verses 1 and 2 and verses 17 to 19;

St. Luke: Chapter 19, verses 28 to 48;

St. John: Chapter 12, verses 12 to 15.

3   Write an account of another incident which occurred on Palm Sunday.

4   In England, the Pussy Willow (*Salix caprea* – also known as the Goat Willow and the Great Sallow) is traditionally used to decorate churches on Palm Sunday. Make a collection of willow and laurel twigs. Draw and colour the beautiful, golden, fluffy catkins of the Pussy Willow.

5   Find out, and list, the countries where palm trees grow. Put their names on a map of the world.

6   Read the twelfth chapter of Exodus and write in your own words an account of what happened at the first Passover.

7   Many years ago, Dorothy L. Sayers wrote a radio play called 'The Man Born to be King', and in those days many people complained because an actor represented the voice of Jesus. Borrow the play from a library and with your friends read the trial scenes from it as though you were broadcasting.

8   Using the Gospel story, write a scene from a Passion play. Perhaps you can persuade some of your friends to join in presenting it to another class in the school.

9   Donkeys were used a great deal at the time when Jesus lived. Find out what you can about donkeys and why they were more popular than horses in Palestine.

5. The Week before Easter

The week before Easter begins on Palm Sunday and is called *Holy Week*. It is the last week in Lent and in it Christians remember all the crowded events of the last days of Jesus on earth. It was such an important week that Matthew, Mark, Luke and John took up a quarter of their gospels writing about it. It is the saddest time of the Christian year when churches hold many services and prayer-meetings. Altars are stripped of their coverings, ornaments and flowers to add to the atmosphere of sadness and mourning.

Jesus spent the week in teaching and discussions with the Jewish Leaders who refused to believe that he was the Messiah, the promised deliverer. They were angry with Jesus and accused him of pretending to be God's Son and Messenger. On the Thursday of the week, Jesus and his disciples met in an upper room to have supper and celebrate the Passover. As the roads were very dusty it was usual in those days for servants to wash the feet of the guests in the house. The disciples were astonished when Jesus, their Master, himself washed and dried the disciples' feet.

During the meal Jesus told his friends that one of them would betray him and hand him over to the Romans. He also warned them that he would be killed but he would return again. The unleavened bread was broken and shared, the wine was passed round and the Last Supper ended. They sang one of the psalms and then

20

'*The Last Supper*'

went outside into a big garden called Gethsemane. One of the disciples, Judas, was disappointed that Jesus had not raised an army to overthrow the Roman rulers. It was he who pointed Jesus out to a crowd of armed men, who had come to capture him, by greeting him with a kiss. The soldiers led Jesus away to be tried whilst all the disciples ran away frightened.

These are some of the events which Christians recall on the Thursday of Holy Week which is known as *Maundy Thursday*. This name comes from a Latin word meaning a 'commandment' because it was on this day that Jesus gave his disciples a new commandment, or order, to love one another.

The *Royal Maundy* is a custom which began eight hundred years ago and is still carried on today. Purses of money, in the form of special silver coins, are distributed on this day to selected old or poor people by the reigning monarch. The number of coins is always the same number as the years of the reign of the Sovereign. The number of purses distributed to the men and women is always the same as there are years in the Sovereign's age.

This custom used to include an even older one which has now ceased. At one time priests used to put a linen towel round themselves and wash the feet of the faithful. In England some servants, called the Yeomen of the Laundry, used to wash the feet of the poor while the King or Queen watched. One King, James II, did the foot-washing himself in the 1680s, but he was the last monarch to do so. Pope John XXIII revived the custom in 1961, after an interval of twenty-three years.

The events of Good Friday are well known. After his trial Jesus was cruelly treated and was made to carry his cross to a hill called Golgotha, often referred to as Calvary, overlooking the city of Jerusalem. It was here that Jesus was crucified, which was the Roman way of punishing criminals by nailing them to a cross (crux) and leaving them to die. Since that day its anniversary has been spent quietly by Christians. During the reign of Constantine in the fourth century AD it was set aside as a holiday, and it has been a public holiday in the British Isles for many years. In some churches the bells are tied up so that they cannot ring and the inside of the buildings is kept stripped and bare of decorations. A three-hour service is usually held from midday to three o'clock in the afternoon and the priest normally preaches a series of sermons about the words Jesus spoke while he was hanging from the cross.

The cross on which Jesus was crucified is said to have been made from the poplar or aspen tree, which some people believe still shivers in horror at what happened

'Christ of St. John of the Cross'

on the first Good Friday. Good Friday was thought to be an unlucky day on which to work, particularly for miners and fishermen. Many people did not like to use iron tools or nails on that day, because of the nails used for Christ's hands and feet. The superstition that '13' is an unlucky number is said to date from the Last Supper when thirteen sat down to eat. It is thought that, if thirteen people are at table, one will soon die. However, the superstition existed before the Last Supper. In Norse mythology, Loki, the spirit of Strife, appeared when twelve gods were at a feast. His appearance started a quarrel which caused the death of Baldur, the gods' favourite.

Many children wonder why the day is called 'Good' Friday if it was such a sad day in the life of Christians. One explanation is that the day was once known as 'God' Friday just as the word 'goodness' used to be 'godness'. Another explanation Christians give is that it really was Good Friday because Jesus gave his life to wipe out the sins of mankind.

There is a custom which used to be widespread but seems now to take place only in a part of Liverpool. Early on Good Friday morning children appear in the streets carrying a figure which looks like Guy Fawkes but is really supposed to be Judas. The children knock on bedroom windows with the figure on a pole and shout 'Judas wants a penny for his breakfast'. The people in the houses usually throw out their pennies to get rid of the children. After visiting a number of houses, the children start to burn Judas on a bonfire in the middle of the street. This dangerous practice is normally stopped by a policeman who comes along to put out the fire and carry the Judas away. It is a common sight to see children following a policeman on his way to the police station shouting 'Judas' at him.

24

Holy Saturday or Easter Eve is the last day of Lent and is the day before Easter Sunday. Many people call it Easter Saturday but this is not correct as it is not possible to have a day called Easter before Easter has arrived.

After Jesus had died, a good man called Joseph, who came from the Judaean town of Arimathaea, asked Pontius Pilate, the Roman Governor, if he could have the body of Jesus. Joseph's request was granted and he took the body and put it in a new tomb which had been cut out of the rock. A big stone was rolled in front of the tomb and Roman soldiers were put on guard so that the body should not be moved. The Sabbath was about to begin. In many Christian churches throughout the world a vigil or watch is kept during the night until Easter Day arrives.

Things to do

1   Count the number of chapters in the four gospels and then decide how many of them tell the story of Jesus' last days in Jerusalem. What *fraction* of the gospels deals with Holy Week?

2   Draw or paint a picture to illustrate an event during that week. Suggestions: a Roman soldier; a silhouette of the Crucifixion; the crowd around the fire when Peter said he didn't know Jesus; on the road to Calvary.

3   What seven sentences did Jesus say on the cross? What do they tell you about the sort of person Jesus was?

4   Make a model of either the Crucifixion or the tomb in which Jesus was buried.

5   The last twenty-four hours of the life of Jesus were packed with incidents. Make a list of these in the order in which they happened.

6   Read one of the gospel stories connected with this week. You will find them in:
   St. Matthew's Gospel: Chapters 21 to 27;
   St. Mark's Gospel: Chapters 11 to 15;
   St. Luke's Gospel: Chapters 22 and 23;
   St. John's Gospel: Chapters 13 to 19.

7   Different members of the class can write an account of the part played in these events by one of the following: Barabbas, Caiaphas, Herod, Jesus, Peter, Judas, Pontius Pilate, a Roman soldier, some other person. The accounts can be combined in a folder or booklet with a good title.

8   Roman Governors had to write official reports of events which took place in their provinces. Write a letter which Pontius Pilate might have written to Caesar stating what had happened in Jerusalem during this eventful week.

6. Easter Day

After Jesus had died his body was taken down from the cross by two of his followers, Joseph and Nicodemus. They buried him hastily in the tomb before the great Festival Sabbath began as darkness fell on the Friday evening. The body was wrapped in a linen sheet and placed on a shelf cut in the wall at one side of the tomb.

It was usual for bodies to be treated with ointment and spices but there had been no time to do this before the Sabbath began and it would have to wait until the Sabbath was over. Three women had followed Jesus from Galilee: Mary of Magdala, Joanna, and Mary the mother of James. These three had helped Joseph and Nicodemus with the burial, so they knew exactly where Jesus' body had been buried. They prepared their ointment and spices and waited for the Sabbath to end.

'The Risen Christ'

At dawn the next day the two Marys and Joanna set off out of the city to finish the last rites of burial. As they hurried along they were worrying about how they would be able to roll away the great boulder from the entrance to the tomb. They reached the garden and stopped in amazement: the stone had been rolled away and the tomb was open. Nervously they entered the cave but the body of Jesus was not inside. The women ran back to Jerusalem to report what had happened to Peter, John and the rest of the disciples.

The disciples had hidden away since they had seen Jesus seized in the garden of Gethsemane, because they were afraid that they too would be arrested. They must have felt very sad: not only had their Master failed to set up the Kingdom they had discussed together but he was now dead. Suddenly the women who had returned from the garden rushed in with the news that their Master had risen and the tomb was empty. The story seemed to the disciples to be so unlikely that they said it was nonsense and refused to believe it. Peter and John were finally persuaded to go to the tomb and see for themselves what had happened. They too found the tomb empty except for the grave-clothes. In a confused state they returned home. That evening, as they were discussing the day's events, they suddenly found Jesus standing amongst them.

The disciples who had scattered after the death of Jesus soon reassembled and one by one they claimed they had seen Jesus alive. This news had a dramatic effect on his followers. Whereas on Good Friday they had been frightened, they were now excited and unafraid. The early Christians were full of courage and many of them were later put to death for their beliefs. This great faith and the trials they had undergone are the main reasons that a thousand million people follow the teachings of

Jesus today. The most important part of these is based on his rising from the dead which is known as Christ's Resurrection./

The astonishing events of that weekend are remembered each Easter as Christians celebrate the resurrection of Jesus with great rejoicing. Millions of them flock on Easter Day to churches which are decorated with candles and flowers, and where the priests and altars are dressed in white. There they hear again the events of the first Easter Day and sing psalms and hymns which are full of happiness and hope.

In some countries Roman Catholics put out the lights in their churches on Good Friday and, on Easter Eve, make a new fire to light the big Easter or Paschal candle. This great candle is used in Easter services as a symbol of the risen Jesus being the light of the world. The candle has symbols of Jesus engraved on it and is studded with grains of incense so that it will smell when it burns on Easter Sunday. After being blessed on Holy Saturday, it is placed on the left of the altar until Ascension Day. The candle is lit on Easter Day and on all the Sundays and Saints' days during that time. All the other candles in the church are lit from it on Easter Sunday. In some places people light their own candles from the great Paschal candle and carry them home to be used on special occasions.

There is an old belief that the sun danced with joy when Jesus rose from the dead on Easter morning, and people used to climb hills to see the sun dance and hold sunrise services.

On many hilltops in Northern and central Europe bonfires are still set alight on Easter Day. People gather round the fires to sing Easter hymns and rejoice because of Jesus Christ's resurrection.

'Light of the World'

Things to do

1 Moslems have their weekly holy day on Fridays whilst the Jewish Sabbath is on Saturdays. Why do Christians keep Sunday as their holy day?

2 How are candles used in church celebrations on Easter Day? What is the reason for this?

3 Many Christians have been punished and put to death for their beliefs. Write the story of one of them.

4   Read the accounts of the first Easter Day in the following passages from the gospels:
St. Matthew: Chapter 27, verses 55 to 66 and Chapter 28, verses 1 to 10;
St. Luke: Chapter 23, verses 49 to 56 and Chapter 24, verses 1 to 11;
St. John: Chapter 19, verses 38 to 42 and Chapter 20, verses 1 to 25.

5   At the beginning of chapter 20 of St. John's gospel Peter and another disciple are mentioned. Who was the other one? Why do you think so?

6   What part did the women friends of Jesus play in the events of the first Easter Day?

7   Imagine that you were one of the friends of Jesus in that room when news was brought of the resurrection. Describe what happened and what your own feelings were.

8   The scene at the tomb would make a fine play which you could write and record on tape. The characters will be the two Marys, Joanna, Peter, John, the 'gardener' and the angel.

9   Flowers play an important part in decorating churches on Easter Day. Try your hand at arranging some flowers to decorate your classroom or home.

7. Easter Games

Outdoor games have always become much more popular with the coming of spring, longer hours of daylight and the promise of better weather. What we now regard as children's games were long ago played mainly by adults who have carried on the custom in many places.

Marbles is a game which was played very seriously in the north of England, and in Surrey and Sussex. The marble season started on Ash Wednesday and finished on Good Friday. In the southern counties of England the last day of the season was called *Marble Day* and the game was played only by grown men. At Tinsley Green, near Crawley in Sussex, a championship match is still held on Good Friday. The games are played every year and the custom is thought to have started three hundred years ago.

Tinsley Green Marble Match

32

Spring is the time when girls now take out their skipping ropes but it is a pastime which was once enjoyed by everybody. Skipping is a very old activity which hundreds of years ago was supposed to have the magical power of making the seeds grow in springtime. In the Middle Ages people used to go out on Palm Sunday and Good Friday to skip on raised mounds called 'Barrows', which were ancient burial places.

Shrovetide was a popular time for playing ball-games, with football as one of the traditional sports. This was a wild and rowdy game with none of the rules which have been drawn up now. Like other games, football was played in the streets and often lasted all day until one of the sides managed to get the ball into its *own* goal miles away from the kick-off point. Players often ended up with kicks on the shins, bruised bodies and broken limbs.

Easter Monday is still called *Ball Monday* by some of the older people in Oxfordshire. This is because of the great number of ball-games, such as bowls, stoolball, football and handball, which used to be played on this day. Ball-games and scrambles seem to go back to pagan times but no one seems to know why.

Other games were played during the Easter holiday. These included 'knur and spell', 'ninepins', 'tipcat' and 'prisoners' bars'. A knur is a small, hard, pot ball and a spell is a machine with a spring which sends the ball into the air. The object of the game is to hit the knur as far as possible with a wooden stick with a small club on the end.

Tipcat is a similar game played with a shaped piece of wood called a cat which is struck in the air by a wooden stick, the catstaff. Prisoners' bars is now a children's

33

game which is also called 'prisoners' base', 'chevy chase', 'chivy' or just 'base'. It was played seriously by adults until about a hundred and thirty years ago, but it was said that it lost its popularity because of a game called cricket which was becoming popular in the south of England!

Things to do

1   Marbles used to be made of terracotta or clay but are now almost always made of glass. Can you describe how to play a game of marbles?

2   Until recently children used to bowl iron, steel or wooden hoops along the pavements in spring with a stick or hook. Why do you think this game is very rarely played now?

3   How many skipping games do you know? Make a list of them and write the words of the rhymes or songs which go with them.

4   Write a set of rules for one of these games: knur and spell, ninepins or tipcat. The game of tipcat is known by different names in various parts of the country; for example, in Yorkshire it is called 'nipsy' and is played with a shaped piece of wood and a special stick.

5   What games are played in spring where you live? Are any of the games very old?

6   Read how to play 'prisoners' base' in a book called *Children's Games in Street and Playground* by Peter and Iona Opie (published by OUP). You may also be interested to read about other games which are mentioned in this book.

8. Easter Hares and Rabbits

Many years ago, in ancient Egypt, hares and rabbits were the symbols of birth and new life in spring. Other civilisations in olden times also looked on hares and rabbits as symbols of a new moon or as new growth which starts in spring. The Saxon goddess of the Dawn and Spring was *Eastre*, whose sacred animal was the hare. Christians later adopted the hare as the symbol for Easter and fixed its festival from the time of the full moon.

Hares are animals which have a coat of brown, grey or white fur. They have long ears with black tips, a split upper lip and short bushy tail which is easy to see when they run on their powerful hind legs. Adult hares can grow to a length of over half a metre (20 inches). They eat plants and go out at night to search for their food. At dawn they return to their homes which are not burrows but grassy hollows, called 'forms', which are usually sheltered by rocks or tree stumps.

Hares mate when they are about six months old and each year the females produce two or three litters of two to five young, which are called 'leverets' during their first year of life. They are born completely covered with hair and can open their eyes at birth. They stay quiet and concealed in their form whilst their parents are out looking for food. Hares are very active in spring and act in an excited manner; they jump up in the air, twist their bodies and land to thump the ground with their long back legs.

Wild rabbits are not as big as hares: they are about 20 to 36 centimetres (8 to 14 inches) long and weigh about 1 to $2\frac{1}{4}$ kilograms (2 to 5 pounds). Their soft, thick fur and short, fluffy tails vary in colour and can be brown, grey, white or a mixture of all of them. Rabbits have long ears which they can move together or separately to catch the faintest sounds. Their eyes are set on the side of their heads so that they can see things at the side of them or behind. They twitch their noses continually and depend for their safety on their keen sense of smell.

Rabbits do not walk or run but hop on their hind legs using their front ones to balance. They dig burrows in which they live and shelter their young which are naked and blind at birth and cannot move about. The female, which is larger than the male, produces a litter of four or five young at a time several times a year. They eat plants and can often be seen feeding near hedges at dusk.

Many children keep pet rabbits in hutches in their gardens and these animals tend to be longer, heavier and live five times longer than the wild ones. Rabbits will normally live for about a year if they are unharmed but they are often hunted for food and for their skins. The name for rabbit fur is 'coney'. Fur from Angora rabbits is spun into soft, warm wool for sweaters and cardigans, whilst felt is made from squeezing rabbit fur together with other kinds of fur.

Rabbits are more common than hares and people are often muddled about which is which. This accounts for the fact that some Easter legends about the animals are sometimes about hares and sometimes about rabbits.

There is a German legend that a poor mother preserved

and dyed some eggs during a time when there was very little to eat. She hid them in a nest to provide a meal for her children to eat on Easter Day. The family went to search for the food on Easter morning and, just as they approached the place where it was hidden, a big rabbit jumped away from the nest of eggs. The story soon spread among children in Europe that it is rabbits which bring eggs at Easter.

The children in Yugoslavia still search farm stables to find eggs in the straw of a hare's nest. In Germany and Hungary children collect their eggs in a basket decorated with the figure of a hare. When people from parts of Europe settled in the United States of America, they took these stories with them and in that country today it is the 'Easter bunny' which is supposed to bring Easter eggs and presents.

In former times English children used to search corners of their houses and gardens for the eggs which the Easter hare had hidden. Although the custom is now dying out there are still reminders of the traditions connected with the Easter hare. Hunting the hare was a popular pastime in the Midlands some years ago.

Things to do

1 It is often said that someone is 'as mad as a March hare'. What do you think it means?

2 Make a list of the differences between hares and rabbits under the headings: appearance, size, food, home, young, how they move and their behaviour.

3 Write a short guide on 'How to look after pet rabbits'.

4 Draw this hare and rabbit and colour them. Which is which?

5 The March Hare appears in chapter seven of a book called *Alice's Adventures in Wonderland* by Lewis Carroll, (published by Macmillan Children's Books). The White Rabbit is also in this story which is well worth reading.

6 Hounds are used in hare-coursing to chase and catch hares. What do you think about this sport? Can you ask your teacher to arrange a debate on the subject? The members of the class will have to speak for a short time on whether they support or oppose hare-coursing.

7 Read *Watership Down* by Richard Adams, (published by Penguin Books). It is an exciting story about rabbits and won an award for children's fiction in 1972.

9. Easter Eggs

Most children look forward to receiving, and eating, at least one chocolate egg but the custom of having eggs at the great spring festivals began hundreds of years before the first Easter. Eleven hundred years ago the Chinese exchanged eggs which had been dyed red. The ancient Egyptians dyed eggs green and gave them to their friends in spring.

The Persians used to believe that the earth had hatched from a giant egg and so they held all eggs in great esteem. To the ancient Greeks, and all pagans, eggs represented the return of new life to the world of nature in spring. Most of these peoples coloured the eggs red because this was the symbol of life itself.

The early Christians were quick to adopt the egg as a symbol of Jesus rising from the tomb and to them it represented the beginning of new life. In the country we now call Iraq they had coloured eggs at Easter, and in many Europe countries people exchanged eggs to show their joy at the resurrection of Jesus. In Poland there is a story that Mary painted eggs red to amuse the baby Jesus, and for many years Polish mothers have continued to do the same for their own children.

A Romanian legend tells of Mary bringing a gift of eggs to the soldiers at the foot of the cross in the hope that they would be kind to her son. The story goes on to say that his blood flowed over the eggs and so made them red. In the Middle Ages Christians were glad to eat eggs again at Easter as they were one of the foods they had been forbidden to eat during Lent. Coloured eggs have remained a popular Easter gift throughout the years and, as recently as 1935, a model dairy at Caterham in Surrey sent dyed eggs to its customers on Easter Day.

The modern Easter egg is shaped like a real egg. It is made of chocolate or sugar, and is often wrapped in a gaily coloured cardboard case. Sometimes eggs are filled with chocolates or sweets, and cardboard eggs can be bought which have a small gift inside. Chocolate eggs were first sold just over a hundred years ago and, although they are very popular, they have not completely taken the place of the traditional Easter eggs. These were hard-boiled hens' eggs which people used to give their friends on Easter Day. Sometimes the eggs had messages, mottoes and dates on them; some were very fancy hollow eggs with a window at one end through which pictures could be seen. These were very popular during the last century and were polished and preserved in ale-glasses for many years.

Although real eggs are no longer exchanged in Britain, the customary Easter breakfast is still boiled eggs which have been decorated in some way. There is a superstition among many people that the egg-shell must be broken up after the egg has been eaten, so that fairies which live in the land cannot use the shells as boats and sail away in them. This custom may have begun with the Romans who used to break up the shells of eaten eggs so that they could not be used for making magic.

Boiled eggs are served decorated with beautiful patterns, or dyed in bright colours which do not affect the taste of the eggs. There are many ways of colouring eggs by using natural dyes from flowers, plants, vegetables and leaves. Boiling eggs with onion skins turns them yellow or brown. Spinach leaves turns them green, and gorse flowers make them yellow. Cochineal gives them a scarlet colour and some kinds of bark turn eggs purple.

Dyes can also be bought from shops and can be used to make eggs any required colour. A most attractive effect can be achieved by writing on eggs with candle or crayon with the result that the dye does not colour the parts covered by the wax. Felt-tipped pens can also be used to decorate eggs with patterns or with funny faces.

In Europe eggs are decorated with all kinds of patterns. In Hungary people paint flowers on their eggs and the Russians used to decorate theirs with pictures of Jesus and the Saints. The Poles paint crosses and fishes, and people in Czechoslovakia are particularly clever at designing Easter egg patterns.

41

A famous jeweller, called Peter Carl Fabergé, was well-known for the Easter eggs he used to make out of precious metals and jewels. He lived from 1846 to 1920 and was Russian, although his parents were French.

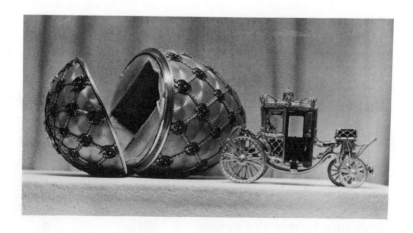

Russian china factories had made eggs for a hundred years before, but Fabergé made one for the Czar, Alexander III, to give to his wife one Easter. This gift was shaped like a real egg. In later years presents were often put in egg-shaped cases. One of these was a clock with a cockerel which rose on the hour and flapped its wings. The Czar's gift to his wife in 1884 became a tradition in the Royal family and was later copied by other wealthy families. Some people often give Easter 'eggs' which are not eggs at all but are Easter presents.

In Britain there are still many customs which are connected with Easter eggs or 'Pace-eggs' as they are called in many places. (Pace, or Peace, comes from the English word Paschal which had its origins in the Hebrew term for the Passover). Sometimes the Pace-eggs are begged, or thrown in the air, or rolled or broken. As these egg ceremonies started many hundreds of years ago they must have had magical or religious meanings but have now become interesting games and pastimes.

At one time a popular game in Britain, France and other parts of the world, was to throw eggs up in the air and catch them. The one who dropped an egg had to pay a forfeit. One game still played is 'egg-shackling'. Players hold a hard-boiled egg and try to break the eggs of other players which they keep if they succeed.

'Egg-rolling' takes place on Easter Sunday or Monday in various parts of the British Isles and also in Switzerland. The game consists of rolling brightly coloured hard-boiled eggs down hillsides and then eating the eggs if they get cracked or broken. Some people believe that the custom began in pagan times as a sun-festival, whereas others think that there is a connection between rolling eggs and rolling the stone away from the tomb in the garden where Jesus was buried.

The largest Easter egg ever seen weighed 205 kilograms (550 lb) and was made at the Liverpool College of Crafts and Catering in March 1971.

Pace-egging can still be found in many northern counties of England. Nowadays only children take part in the custom but years ago the Pace-eggers, or Jolly-boys, used to go round begging for eggs and acting the Pace-egg Play. This was an Easter version of an old mumming play in which the characters blacked their faces and sewed paper streamers on their clothes. The play is not always acted now although the characters still have their old names such as Betty Brownbags and Old Tosspot.

Things to do

1   In this chapter there is a brief outline of a Romanian legend. Make this into a longer story by describing how Mary heard the news about Jesus, what she decided to do, how she got the eggs, the journey she made to Golgotha, what she saw when she arrived, what she said to the Roman soldiers, what they replied, what happened to the eggs and what Mary did afterwards.

2   Write an account of how people decorated their real Easter eggs to give to their friends more than a hundred years ago.

3   Here are some suggestions for decorating hard-boiled eggs:
(**a**) Paint faces on the eggs with felt-tipped pens and dress them in funny hats.
(**b**) Write your name in candle wax or crayon on a warm egg and then paint it all over with a coloured ink.
(**c**) Cover the warm eggs with different coloured wax crayons so that the colours all run into each other.

(**d**) Make a stencil of a chicken, rabbit, hare or pattern and use it to make a picture on the egg with felt-tipped pens.

(**e**) With the help of an adult try dyeing eggs using onion skins, spinach leaves or cochineal.

4   Describe what happens in egg-rolling games. Why do you think this custom started?

5   What part did the egg play in the old spring festivities? How did the customs of using eggs start and why did the early Christians adopt them?

6   What is 'Pace-egging'? Describe what happens and try to make up an egg-begging verse.

7   How did 'Pace-egg' get its name?

8   Try to blow an egg and decorate it. Pierce both ends of the egg carefully with a needle to break the yolk. Blow gently from one end of the egg until the contents slowly come out of the hole at the other end. Rinse the egg out well. Paint or decorate the shell using varnish to strengthen it. Stick on tiny leaves or flowers or glue on fabric, lace, wool, sequins or beads to make an attractive pattern.

10. Easter Clothes

Many years ago the season of Lent was far more strictly kept than it is now. It was a time of fasting, mourning and sober living even to the point of wearing dull and drab clothes. These were often sprinkled with ashes to imitate the Old Testament custom of wearing sack-cloth and ashes as a sign of sorrow. It was natural, therefore, that when Lent was over, people were glad to change out of their dusty old clothes into gayer ones and to wear new outfits after the cold winter months.

The tradition of wearing new clothes also arose out of a superstition summed up by an old English rhyme:

'At Easter let your clothes be new
Or else be sure you will it rue.'

It was also believed that, if people did not wear something new to church on Easter Sunday, the birds would let their droppings fall on them! It is interesting that the superstition has changed over the years as now it is thought to be lucky if bird droppings fall on someone wearing new clothes.

Many people still think of Easter as a good time to buy and wear new clothes and to have new spring outfits in which to go to church. The most popular idea following this custom was to wear a new hat for Easter. In former years hats were much more commonly worn than they are now, and neither men nor women would dream of going out bareheaded. A new hat therefore became the most proper and noticeable garment one could have. Hats could be very fancy and it became fashionable among ladies to wear most extravagant 'Easter bonnets'. Poorer women, who could not afford a complete new hat, used to buy new trimmings and decorate their old hat with lace, ribbons, flowers and feathers to make it look new.

Some years ago it became popular to hold Easter parades in order that adults and children could show off their finery. One such parade is normally held each spring in London's Battersea Park and is often combined with a parade of vintage cars. The Easter parade has become a popular tradition in many cities in the United States on Easter Sunday. The most famous is on New York's Fifth Avenue where the traffic is stopped to allow the well-dressed New Yorkers to show off their Easter outfits and bonnets.

Easter Parade, Battersea Park

Things to do

1   You will enjoy making an Easter bonnet which can be of any design and as ridiculous or extravagant as possible. Here is a suggestion:

From thin card cut out these shapes. The rectangle must be long enough to go round the inside of the brim.

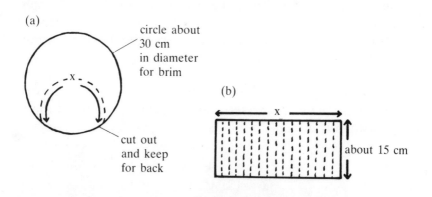

(a)

circle about 30 cm in diameter for brim

x

cut out and keep for back

(b)

x

about 15 cm

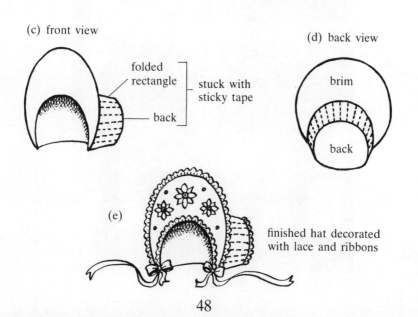

(c) front view

folded rectangle

stuck with sticky tape

back

(d) back view

brim

back

(e)

finished hat decorated with lace and ribbons

Tape the three pieces together and decorate the bonnet with tissue paper, ribbons, lace or any other material.

2 Have a class parade of Easter bonnets and hats. Everyone should make a hat and a prize could be given for the most sensational one.

3 On a more serious note, 'Hats through the Ages' provides an interesting project; what you find out could be made into a class booklet.

4 A few years ago a man invented something called 'Open-ended tests' in which pupils had to give all the uses they could think of for a well-known object. How many uses are there for a hat? Here are two:
(a) Fill it with water and give a dog a drink.
(b) Use it as a wastepaper basket.
Make a list of all the other uses you can think of.

5 Gentlemen used to raise their hats to ladies in the street when out walking. How do you think the custom started? Why is the practice dying out?

6 Design a new Easter outfit for yourself which can be an extraordinary creation or something you would really like to wear. Designs can be stuck on to a frieze to make an Easter parade.

11. Easter Food

Eating plays such an important part in our lives that it is natural that many of the Easter customs are concerned with food. The season of Lent used to be a time of fasting or going without foods such as meat, butter, eggs and cream. The fast was kept very seriously indeed by all Christians, and it is little wonder that people used to enjoy as many luxuries as possible in great quantities before Lent began.

Each day of Shrovetide was called after a special food which it was the custom to eat on that day. The Saturday before Ash Wednesday was called 'Egg Saturday' in many places because of the custom of finishing off the eggs on that day. In Lincolnshire it was 'Bursting Saturday' when people used to eat a very thick crumbly pancake known as frying-pan pudding. The following Monday had various names apart from Shrove Monday. In the north of England it was 'Collop Monday', a time for eating a fried concoction of eggs, bacon and any other meat which was left in the house. In Cornwall it was known as 'Peasen Monday' when it was the custom to eat thick pea soup.

The real feast-day was, of course, Shrove Tuesday: the last day foods could be eaten that would be forbidden during the next six weeks. We have already seen, in chapter 2, that the pancake was the customary dish on this day. Long before Christianity began, a small wheat cake had played a part in the spring festivals and some people believe that this was the origin of the pancake. Although the making of pancakes is no longer an excuse for using up the eggs and fat, the pleasant custom of eating them is still observed and Pancake Day is as popular as ever.

50

Shrove Tuesday has many other names and 'Fastern's E'en' (or Even) describes well what it once was: the eve of the fast. In Scotland it was 'Beef Day', 'Brose Day' or 'Bannock Tuesday'. Everyone who could afford it ate beef on this day especially farmers who believed that failure to have a beef dinner would lead to the death of their cattle.

Brose was a kind of thick soup in which various small articles were hidden on this day. Young people used to dip their spoons into the huge bowl and try to find the charms which would foretell the future. A ring meant the finder would soon marry, a coin was the sign of riches in the near future, and a thimble was supposed to mean there would be no wedding for that person for at least a year.

Another delicacy on this day was fitness cock, which was an oatmeal and suet dumpling shaped like a bird. Bannock Night was the time for baking pancake-like loaves made of oatmeal, eggs, salt and milk, or flour, eggs and sugar. They were baked over a round iron

51

plate hung over the fire and everybody who was not married had to take part in cooking them. Friends and neighbours usually gathered together to eat the bannocks, one of which contained a charm to foretell the future of whoever chose it.

At Baldock, in Hertfordshire, Shrove Tuesday used to be known as 'Doughnut Day', because doughnuts fried in lard, used to be eaten on that day. Doughnuts are still eaten on the same day in Vienna, the capital of Austria, during the Carnival. Small currant buns in the shape of shells used to be sold in the streets and bakers' shops of Norwich on Shrove Tuesday. In these, and many other ways, people cleared their larders of forbidden foods before the beginning of Lent, but in some parts of the north of England fritters with currants in were still being eaten on 'Fruttors Thursday', the day after Ash Wednesday!

By tradition, the Sundays in Lent were not strictly for fasting and this may account for the fact that some delicacies were eaten on those days. The fourth Sunday in Lent, Mothering Sunday, was the day when simnel cakes were eaten and a special dinner was arranged with dishes such as roast veal or lamb, suet dumplings, rice puddings and custard.

Passion Sunday, the fifth in Lent, used to be called 'Care' or 'Carling Sunday' and the name is still used in Scotland and in the north of England. On this day it was customary to eat carlings (grey, dried peas). These were soaked in water overnight, seasoned with salt, pepper and vinegar and fried in butter. They were served at the Sunday dinner and were often provided by innkeepers to eat as customers drank their beer.

On the sixth Sunday, Palm Sunday, fig-pies and puddings were eaten and the day was often referred to as Fig Sunday. On the same day, pax (peace) cakes and ale were distributed to the pensioners in three villages in Herefordshire. These were taken round the congregation in church to ensure that everyone would be peaceful and friendly at Easter. The custom began more than four hundred years ago but now the pax cakes are flat wafers which are given out by the Vicar to the congregation as they leave the church. He still says, 'Peace and good neighbourhood' to the parishioners to remind them of the way in which the custom began.

The custom of eating hot-cross buns on Good Friday is still carried on in most British homes, but similar cakes were being made long before the day on which Jesus was crucified. The pagan Greeks and Romans ate small wheaten cakes marked with a cross at the spring festival of Diana, the goddess of hunting. The Saxons, who first appeared about eighteen hundred years ago, ate similar cakes in March many years before that part of Germany had been converted to Christianity.

Two fossilised loaves with crosses on them were found in the ruins of Herculaneum, a town near Naples in Italy, many years after it had been destroyed by a volcano in AD 79. On Good Friday in 1361 similar cakes were given to the poor at St. Alban's Abbey in Hertfordshire and these had become very popular in England by the beginning of the eighteenth century.

At that time housewives used to get up very early in the morning to make round, spiced cakes marked with a cross to be eaten hot at breakfast. Bakers also used to work during the night so that the buns would be ready to sell early on Good Friday morning. In London and in other big towns men were on the streets very early carrying on their heads baskets of buns covered by

white cloths to keep them hot. As the men moved along they called out the cry which later became a popular nursery rhyme:

'Hot-cross buns! Hot-cross buns!
One-a-penny, two-a-penny,
Hot-cross buns!'

Nowadays fewer housewives bake their own buns and these, which are sometimes marked with a dough cross, are usually bought cold from bakers' shops and stores a day or so before Good Friday. The custom is dying out of eating them hot for breakfast and many people now have them toasted for tea. They are, however, still eaten in many parts of the world though people no longer believe, as they once did, that buns cooked on Good Friday can cure diseases such as diarrhoea and whooping cough.

The original cross, whose history goes back to pagan times, now has a special meaning for Christians as it represents the cross on which Jesus died and has come to be the Easter symbol of his victory over death.

After the Lenten fast it was natural that people in former days should want to eat well on Easter Sunday. To mark the end of Lent those who could afford them ate rich foods like duck, veal and pork with sage, parsley and thyme stuffing followed by spinach tarts, custards and cream. The traditional Easter dinner was roast lamb, mint sauce and green peas served on tables decorated with biscuits and cakes in the shape of a lamb. This recalls the Jewish custom of sacrificing the paschal lamb during the Passover ceremony in the temple at Jerusalem. Early Christians looked on the offering of the paschal lamb as forecasting the sacrifice of Jesus on the cross. In verse 29 of the first chapter of St. John's gospel the writer tells the story of John the Baptist seeing Jesus coming towards him. 'Look,' he

says, 'there is the Lamb of God; it is he who takes away the sins of the world.' So at Easter, Christ is compared to a lamb which is innocent but still is killed.

Things to do

1 Lamb used to be the most popular meat eaten on Easter Sunday. What is the favourite meal now on that day?

2 Of all the foods mentioned in this chapter, which is the one you like most and the one you like least? Why?

3 What are the ingredients of
(a) fitness cock (b) bannocks (c) brose?

4 Why was Passion Sunday sometimes called Carling Sunday?
What was eaten on this day in Scotland and the north of England?

5 What kinds of food did people eat
(a) before Lent (b) during Lent (c) after Lent?

6 Make a list of all the different names for Shrove Tuesday. Why did this day have several names?

7 How do we know that hot-cross buns have a very long history?

12. Easter Music

S ome of the world's finest music has been written
  about the first Easter and the days which led up to
  it. This music was mainly written to tell the gospel
story of the suffering of Jesus. It is known as *Passion
music* and was first sung in the fourth century. Since
that time much sacred music has been played and sung
in Holy Week and, during the past three hundred
years, this has taken the form of 'oratorios' and 'cantatas'. These musical compositions are performed by
soloists, a choir and an orchestra but have no action,
scenery or costumes. A cantata is a kind of short
oratorio.

The greatest 'passions' ever composed were written by
Johann Sebastian Bach, who lived between 1685 and
1750. Bach was born at Eisenach in Germany and was
the son of a violinist. His parents died when he was ten
and he was brought up by his elder brother who taught
him to play the clavicord and harpsicord. While he was
still a boy Bach secretly copied his brother's organ

J.S. Bach

music at night with the result that he injured his eyes and later became blind. When he was eighteen Bach joined an orchestra as a violinist and later became an organist. As well as bringing up a family of twenty children Bach was a musician and conductor, and wrote hundreds of compositions. These included three hundred pieces for choirs and the magnificent Passions according to St. John and St. Matthew which were written in 1723 and 1729.

Passion hymns tell, in words and music, the events of Palm Sunday and Good Friday. Some of these are very old: St. Theodulph of Orleans wrote this hymn in the ninth century and it was translated into English about one hundred and fifty years ago.

'All glory, laud and honour
To thee, Redeemer, King,
To whom the lips of children
Made sweet hosannas ring.'

Another favourite Palm Sunday hymn was written by H.H. Millman who lived from 1791 to 1868:

'Ride on! ride on in majesty!
Hark all the tribes hosanna cry;
Thine humble beast pursues his road
With palms and scattered garments strowed.'

Mrs. C.F. Alexander (1823–95), who wrote *All things bright and beautiful* and *Once in Royal David's city*, also wrote this sad hymn about the first Good Friday:

'There is a green hill far away,
Without a city wall.
Where the dear Lord was crucified
Who died to save us all.'

Isaac Watts (1674–1748) did not like the hymns sung at that time and decided to write better ones himself. Born in Southampton, England, he learned Latin, Greek and Hebrew as a child and had always been good at making up verses. There is a story that this annoyed his father so much that he decided to spank his son for being cheeky. As he was put over his father's knee for a hiding, Isaac cried out:

'Pray, father, do some pity take,
And I no more will verses make.'

As a young man Watts became a clergyman and was well-known as a great preacher. He wrote seven hundred and sixty hymns. Many of these are still sung all over the world. Watts died in 1748 and there is a memorial to him in Westminster Abbey. One of his hymns, which has been described as the finest one in

*Memorial to I. Watts
in Westminster Abbey*

the English language, is about Good Friday:

'When I survey the wondrous Cross,
On which the Prince of Glory died,
My richest gain I count but loss,
And pour contempt on all my pride.'

There are very many Easter hymns and the earliest of them were written thirteen hundred years ago. The following popular hymn is partly based on a Latin hymn written about six hundred years old:

'Jesus Christ is risen today, Alleluya!
Our triumphant holy day, Alleluya!
Who did once upon the cross, Alleluya!
Suffer to redeem our loss, Alleluya!

There have been very few popular songs about Easter but the most famous one by far is *Easter Parade* by Irving Berlin. He was born Israel Baline in Russia and his family emigrated to the United States of America in 1892 when he was four years old. He attended school for only two years but sold newspapers and sang songs on the streets to make a living. Although he had no musical education he wrote Broadway shows and many famous songs including *God Bless America* and *White Christmas*. He received a gold medal in 1954 from President Eisenhower for his outstanding contribution to popular music.

Things to do

1   Look at the hymns in your school hymn book or in one you may have at home.
Read the ones which describe Palm Sunday and the events of Good Friday.
Make a list of the Easter Sunday hymns.

2   Listen to some of Bach's music, especially pieces from his *Passion according to St. Matthew*.

3   What are oratorios and cantatas?
Why do they have no action, scenery or costumes when they are performed?

4   This is part of the first verse of a hymn which describes children watching Jesus as he rode into Jerusalem:

'They saw the King come riding
Upon his humble beast ...'

Can you finish the verse and make up another verse of the hymn? It can be sung to the tune of *All glory, laud and honour*.

5   From your reference books find out something more about these composers: J.S. Bach, Isaac Watts and Irving Berlin.

6   These musical shows include the Easter story: *Godspell* by Stephen Schwartz and *Jesus Christ Superstar* by Tim Rice and Andrew Lloyd-Webber. Try to listen to some of this music on records or tapes.

13. Easter Art

For three hundred years after the death of Jesus, Christians were treated very badly because they believed that he was the son of God. Some were beaten and imprisoned whilst others were cruelly killed by the Romans. This persecution stopped when the Emperor Constantine allowed Christians to worship in their own way. In AD 330 he moved the capital of the Roman Empire from Rome to the eastern city of Byzantium. He renamed it Constantinople after himself. It is now the largest city in Turkey and is called Istanbul.

The artists in Byzantium had painted pictures of Greek and Roman gods and goddesses such as Apollo and Venus. Now that Christians could worship freely, many of the artists began to paint pictures of scenes from the life of Jesus. At first they were not allowed to show Jesus or his disciples in their paintings because the leaders of the early Church thought that the pictures might be worshipped as idols or gods.

However, by the fifth century, artists were decorating Christian churches with portraits of Jesus and the saints. Soon the fashion spread of making these portraits into *icons* (paintings on panels of wood). For a time the Church ordered them to be destroyed because people seemed to think that the pictures had magical powers to cure illnesses or grant wishes. Ever since, Christians in the Eastern Church have treated icons as holy objects.

As the icons were often placed in dark corners of churches the artists always painted them in bright

colours with bold shapes which could be easily seen. They were sometimes decorated with gold leaf or paint which made them very valuable.

The Roman Empire began to split up in the fifth century and hordes of people called 'Barbarians' over-ran parts of northern Europe. These Barbarians in turn were conquered and converted to Christianity. They could not read or write so the Christian priests used pictures from the life of Jesus to teach them about Christianity. In this way Christian art spread as the Church became more important in people's lives.

Many churches were built during this time which was known as the Middle Ages. The Church owned much land and was very rich so that it could afford to pay artists well. Stained glass became popular but, because the thick heavy walls of churches would be weakened by large pieces of glass, the windows were very small.

To add to the decoration inside the churches, the plaster walls were brightly painted with 'frescoes'. These paintings did not last as long as those on wood or canvas but some have been preserved, such as a few painted in the thirteenth century which can still be seen in the art gallery in Florence and in the Church of St. Francis at Assissi.

'Crucifixion'

Monks in the early monasteries produced lovely hand-written books in the days before printing was invented. These books had beautiful illuminated letters at the beginning of each chapter. One of the most famous illuminated manuscripts is the Book of Kells which contains the four gospels. It was written in Ireland in the eighth century.

Illuminated letter from the Book of Kells

After the Middle Ages came the *Renaissance*, a very important time for art, when artists tried out all sorts of new ideas. Many great painters lived at this time, especially in Italy, and the Easter story was a favourite theme. Giotto's frescoes, for example, include *The Kiss of Judas* and *The Descent from the Cross*. Michelangelo, the famous painter and sculptor, fashioned the wonderful *pietà* which is a statue of Mary mourning over the body of her dead son.

'Kiss of Judas'   'Pietà'

65

El Greco, who lived in Spain, painted large, dramatic and exciting pictures. His works include *Christ Carrying the Cross* and the *Resurrection*.

Religious paintings became less popular after the long Renaissance period. This was especially so among the northern Europeans who did not like them as much as the people in Catholic countries. By this time paintings were no longer needed to teach people about Christianity as more Bibles were printed and more people were able to read. During the seventeenth, eighteenth and nineteenth centuries, most artists preferred to paint portraits, landscapes and scenes from literature and history.

Some artists who painted religious subjects called themselves the Pre-Raphaelites, because they admired the simple style of the Italian painters before Raphael. They often painted pictures which told a story and had a message. *Christ Washing Peter's Feet*, by Ford Madox Brown, is an example of their work and shows Jesus as an ordinary person doing a humble job.

'Christ Washing Peter's Feet'

The painting of religious pictures became less and less popular, and few twentieth century artists painted events from the Easter story. One who did was Salvador Dali, a leading artist in the Surrealist school of painting. Surrealists tried to produce a feeling of magic or mystery in their work and sometimes their paintings were violent and cruel. Dali painted several religious pictures including some of Jesus being crucified.

The English artist Sir Stanley Spencer painted a great number of religious subjects using his Berkshire village of Cookham-on-Thames as a background. The setting of his *Last Supper* is a barn in Cookham and *Christ Carrying the Cross* is painted as though it took place in the village street. He painted several pictures of the first Easter morning and his big *Resurrection* is a masterpiece. This, and many others of his paintings, are in the Tate Gallery in London.

'Christ Carrying the Cross'

67

Things to do

1   Paint a picture about one event in the Easter story and try to make it as real as you can.
Here are some subjects: The Last Supper, Judas betrays Jesus, The Crucifixion, The Empty Tomb.

2   Visit a Christian church or cathedral. Look for stained glass windows, tapestries or stations of the cross which tell part of the Easter story.
What symbol of Christ's death will you find on the altar, outside the church, or on the spire, steeple or tower?
Why do old churches have small windows?

3   At first the early Christian Church did not allow artists to paint pictures of Jesus or the Apostles or the Saints. What was the reason for this?

4   Draw an illuminated capital letter with a tiny picture inside it. Remember to use brightly-coloured inks.

5   What are 'icons'? How were they painted and why was that style used?

6   On a map of Turkey find Istanbul.
What were its former names?
What two continents are separated by the Bosphorus?

7   Long ago, ordinary people could not read or write. How did the priests of the early Christian Church teach them about Christianity apart from reading the Bible to them?

8   Visit your local library and look for some books which are about the history of art.
Read about the life and work of one of the artists which have been mentioned in this chapter.
Can you find any other pictures which illustrate parts of the Easter story?

14. Nature at Easter

Easter cannot be earlier than March 22nd, which is about the time when spring begins. There is an old saying that March comes in like a lion and goes out like a lamb. This shows the sort of change which takes place in the weather during March.

In winter, the sun's rays slant on the northern hemisphere, the half of the world north of the equator, giving us less heat and fewer hours of daylight. In summer the sun's rays are more direct as can be seen from the shorter length of our shadows. In between these two seasons, in spring, we begin to feel the return of the sun's heat. The days become longer and everything in nature begins to produce new life.

Easter flowers are full of colour and brightness after the dullness of winter. As the warmer weather arrives, snowdrops and crocuses begin to come out and there is a feeling that spring is on its way. As Easter is not a fixed date, spring may be well advanced if Easter is late, or hardly under way if Easter is early. Much depends also on whether the previous winter has been mild or harsh.

As spring continues, the sun warms the soil and many flowers bloom. These include primroses, daffodils, narcissi and hyacinths in the garden and cowslips, lady's smocks and marsh marigolds in the meadows. Florists sell flowers from the Channel Islands and Cornwall where spring comes earlier. Arum lilies are ready to come out of the greenhouse and are a certain sign that Easter is here. Lilies are used to decorate churches at

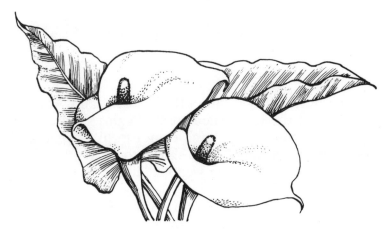

Eastertide and are carried by Easter brides. The Easter lily is tall, with long pointed leaves. The trumpet-shaped flowers have white waxy petals and a fragrant smell.

Green buds start to show on shrubs and trees at this time. Pussy-willow and hazel catkins are among the first to appear and, before long, apple blossom begins to break out in orchards and gardens.

Some people decorate houses and churches with Easter garlands made of ivy, blackthorn and yew. Elder, hawthorn and whitethorn are not used as they are thought to be unlucky.

As plants begin to grow in spring, so the creatures which feed on them start to have their own families because food is plentiful.

Birds, bats and other animals which feed on the increasing number of insects now know that it is time to raise their own young. Some birds, which have spent the winter in Britain, return to their homelands in the cold north. Cuckoos, swallows and warblers return from the south in late spring. Birds begin to make their nests in which to lay their eggs. Many birds will raise two broods before summer is over.

Spring moths, and butterflies such as the yellow brimstone, red admiral and orange-tip, now emerge from their chrysalises. They have been dormant, or sleeping, during the winter. These insects have very short lives. They lay their eggs and these hatch out into caterpillars which spend their days eating the young leaves. Caterpillars do much damage to crops and fruit trees and many are eaten by birds. When caterpillars have eaten their fill they turn into chrysalises by spinning silken cocoons around themselves.

Yellow Brimstone butterfly

In springtime frogs and toads begin to produce their eggs. Croaking loudly they gather together at the pond where they themselves were born. They live mainly on land but must lay their eggs, or spawn, in water. Frog spawn and toad spawn are different in appearance but they develop in similar ways.

When the egg hatches, a tiny tadpole comes out and as it grows it begins to change. Its back legs begin to grow first, then its front legs, and afterwards its tail is absorbed into its body. Soon it will be ready to leave the water as a tiny frog or toad. Many tadpoles are eaten by fish and newts, but toad tadpoles are less tasty than frog tadpoles.

A certain sign of spring is the appearance of lambs which begin to play and leap in meadows and fields. On farms, too, chicks and ducklings are hatching from their eggs. Many people think of lambs and chicks as being a special part of spring and they are often shown on Easter cards.

Animals such as squirrels and hedgehogs, which have been hibernating, now start to breed because there is plenty of food. The growing plants also provide plenty of cover in which they can hide. Foxes are active at this time, and moles begin to raise their litters which feed on the worms which are now multiplying.

Things to do

1 Draw or paint a picture about something in 'Nature at Easter'. This could be a bird feeding its young, ducklings swimming on a pond, lambs in a field or daffodils in the park or garden.

2 Find out and write about an animal in spring which interests you. Think about where it lives, what it eats and what it looks like.

3 Make a class booklet called 'The weather in April'. Pages in it can include surveys about the temperatures and rainfall, pictures about the weather from newspapers, weather forecasts and reports on each day's weather.

4 Make a collection of spring flowers and press some to make a picture. Not all flowers press well, for example daffodils and hyacinths are too bulky, but the following are suitable: primroses, snowdrops, winter aconites, small narcissi, anemones and violets.
Place the flowers between two sheets of blotting paper and arrange the petals carefully. Put some heavy books or weights on top of the blotting paper which will draw the moisture out of the flowers. This makes them papery so be careful when you handle them. After a few days inspect the flowers to see if they are ready to be removed. They can then be arranged on coloured paper or card and glued in place or covered with sticky tape.

5   At the end of the spring term go on a class nature ramble to a wood, field, park or by a river or seashore. Individuals or groups should make a note of different things such as plants, shrubs, trees, flowers, birds, insects, animals, mosses, ferns, amphibians, reptiles and fish.
You can then give a series of short talks on what you have seen to the rest of the class.

6   If you have a bird table, make a note of which birds visit it and on what dates.

7   What would you miss about spring if you were suddenly to move to another country?

8   Collect the spawn of frogs and toads and notice the difference between them.
Keep the spawn in an aquarium or other suitable container and observe the tadpoles as they hatch out. When the tadpoles change into frogs and toads they will need stones on which to emerge from the water. You must then return them to the pond from which the spawn was taken.

9   Write an account of why it becomes warmer and lighter around Easter. Find out about the spring equinox and draw a picture to illustrate what happens on March 20th.

15. Easter in Other Countries

The customs and traditions which are described in this chapter are not all observed in those countries today. They may be followed in parts of various countries but some may have disappeared altogether. There is a pattern which runs through the customs: the merrymaking of Shrove Tuesday, the quietness and seriousness of Holy Week and finally the joy of Easter Day.

All over the world Christians used to celebrate on Shrove Tuesday and there was great rejoicing especially in the south of Europe. The celebrations included feasts, masquerades, parties and carnivals. The word 'carnival' comes from the Latin words *carne vale* which mean 'farewell to meat' or 'put away the meat'.

The carnival, with its merrymaking before the feast to come, had once been a Roman custom. In Roman Catholic countries, and especially in Rome and Venice, carnivals were held for hundreds of years and began on Twelfth Night (January 6th). Feasting and dancing slowly decreased to the three days before Ash Wednesday when people gradually stopped eating those foods, such as meat, which were forbidden in Lent. In time this period of feasting shortened to one day.

In France, and those places where the French have settled, this day is called *Mardi Gras*. This expression means 'Fat Tuesday' and refers to the custom of eating up all the fat and butter before Lent. It is also thought that the term arose from the custom of parading a fat ox, afterwards to be roasted and eaten, through the streets of Paris on that day.

Present-day carnivals consist of processions through the streets of people in masks and fancy dress led by marching bands and musicians. Often the parades include great platforms on wheels, called floats, which are beautifully decorated. The King and Queen of the Carnival lead the procession, sometimes surrounded by giant figures of people in specially made costumes.

The best known carnival parades today are at Nice, in the South of France and at New Orleans in the State of Louisiana, USA. The French colonists introduced the carnival into America about two hundred years ago and it is still very popular in the Southern States.

Carnival in New Orleans

In Germany and Switzerland, Shrove Tuesday is known as *Fastnacht*, which means 'fast-night', when cakes and nuts are eaten. In Denmark and Norway the tradition is for children to decorate branches of the birch tree with gay paper streamers and to pretend to beat their parents with lenten birches until they are rewarded with hot-cross buns.

In Sweden the custom has been to decorate their homes during Lent with birch twigs and chicken feathers. Finnish children receive their Easter eggs on Holy Saturday and eat a traditional cake made with rye meal. Many Scandinavians spend the Easter weekend enjoying winter sports but gather for outdoor services on Easter morning.

Many Christians in Europe spend Lent and Holy Week reverently but there is an interesting custom in Hungary where young people play a fire game on the first Sunday night in Lent. A small hut is built in an open field specially for the occasion. This is set on fire by the girls, and boys heat rings rather like Catherine wheels in the flames. These rings are twirled round on the end of sticks and then sent flying through the darkness. On Easter Monday the boys sprinkle the girls with scented water and are presented with Easter eggs.

Maundy Thursday is sometimes called 'Green Thursday' in Germany because of the custom of colouring eggs green and carrying them around to bring good luck. Children believe that the Easter rabbit hides eggs which they search for in their gardens. Egg-rolling contests are also arranged and the winner can receive as many as a hundred eggs as a prize.

Religious processions are held in Spain on Good Friday when wooden images are carried on platforms in scenes showing the last week of Christ's life. These solemn processions change to happy ones on Easter Day when people dance to jolly music.

The Greeks also have a solemn ceremony to represent Christ's burial. A bier containing a wooden figure of Jesus is carried through the streets as the church congregation form a funeral procession behind. When this returns to church the priest blesses candles and flowers which are distributed to the congregation. On Easter Monday the solemn mood of Holy Week again changes as people dress in traditional costume to dance and sing. In Greece it is the custom for people to tap their red eggs together when they meet on Easter morning and give the greeting 'Christ is risen' which is answered by 'He is risen indeed'.

In many Roman Catholic countries the church bells are silenced from Good Friday to Easter Day. French and Belgian children hear from their mothers the legend that the bells fly to Rome until Easter and drop eggs on the way back. Another legend is that the bells go to Rome to confess to the great bell at St. Peter's. On Easter Sunday the children are told to run out early in the morning to see the angels carrying the bells back to their towers. Many Italians make the journey to Rome to attend the Holy Week services in the famous Basilica (Church) of St. Peter. In Florence there is a strange ceremony on Holy Saturday. A cart is decorated with flowers and fireworks, and pulled by two white oxen through the streets to the door of the cathedral. A wire is connected from the cart to the church altar. From this a lighted firework, in the shape of a dove, rushes along the wire to the cart. The dove lights the fireworks in the cart and zooms back along the wire to the altar. It is considered a good omen if the dove completes its journey both ways before the fireworks explode.

Italian priests bless brightly coloured eggs before the holiday weekend. As many as two hundred of these may be arranged on the centre of the dinner table on Easter Day with other dishes of food around them. Italians often eat rabbit-shaped cakes at Easter.

In the Middle East, Syrian and Armenian Christians have foot-washing ceremonies on Maundy Thursday. Beggars are invited into churches where priests wash their feet and give them gifts. In Jerusalem twelve bishops of the Eastern Orthodox Church, representing the twelve disciples, wash the feet of members of the public. Armenian Christians celebrate Easter Monday by remembering their friends and relatives who are dead. They take food to the places of burial and this is blessed by priests during the ceremony.

In Poland priests bless the eggs and almond cakes which are exchanged among friends on Holy Saturday. Often priests visit the homes of their parishioners to bless the food which will be served at Easter. This has to last throughout Sunday because no food is cooked on that day.

At one time, in parts of the Ukraine, Easter was celebrated for two weeks. The week before Easter was spent in reverence whereas the following week was one of feasting and dancing. This part of Russia was famous for its beautiful Easter eggs which were decorated with pictures of animals, flowers and other scenes. Each village had its own design, such as a church, a cross, a tree, or a priest's robes.

In the Netherlands there is a tradition for children to go from door to door collecting eggs during Holy Week. On Easter Eve young people carry lanterns and join in processions singing Easter songs. When they arrive at the village or town square they spend the evening dancing. On Easter Monday the custom is to play games involving Easter eggs.

In Mexico a favourite game is to break the *piñata*, a jar filled with sweets which the children scramble for when the jar is broken. The piñata is also used at Christmas, but at Easter it is made in the form of a Judas figure. Mexicans fill the streets as soon as it is noon on Holy Saturday, and another of their customs is to beat, hang and burn images of Judas on this day.

In the United States of America many people attend the special services which are held at dawn on Easter Day. Church choirs sing Easter hymns to call church-goers to worship before the sun rises. There are massive congregations at the Punchbowls in Hollywood, California and in Hawaii. Trombones wake up worshippers in Pennsylvania, and throughout the country Christians herald the dawn with cheerful Easter hymns.

Outdoor service in California

80

In the afternoon young people attend Easter parties where attractive tables are laid with place cards and napkins decorated with eggs, chickens and rabbits. During the afternoon, games are organised which always include the traditional Easter egg hunt. Guests have a basket into which they put the eggs which have been hidden around the house and garden. They rush around trying to win the prize which is awarded to the person who finds the most eggs.

All over the world Christians forget for another year the sorrow of Good Friday in the joy of Easter.

Things to do

1   Make a class booklet called 'Easter Abroad', with each child or group writing about a different country. Ask children in your school who have lived abroad to contribute to your booklet.

2   Why are church bells usually silent on Good Friday in Roman Catholic countries?
What legends grew up in Belgium and France as a result of this?

3   Design a place card, napkin or invitation card suitable for use when preparing an Easter party.

4   How did 'Mardi Gras' get its name?
What happens at these celebrations in France and New Orleans?

5   On a duplicated map of Europe write in the names of the countries mentioned in this chapter.
Do you notice where most of them are?

6   Make a papier-mâché piñata in the shape of an Easter egg by using a blown up balloon as the mould. Paste small pieces of newspaper round the balloon until there are several layers. When these are dry, burst the

balloon with a pin. Enlarge the hole to withdraw the balloon and then put sweets inside.

Decorate the egg and hang it in a suitable place so that your friends can try to break it and then scramble for the sweets.

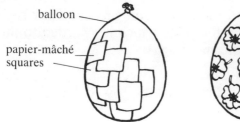

balloon

papier-mâché squares

completed shape

7   Here is a recipe for making Easter biscuits.
You will need:
    225 g (8 oz) flour
    110 g (4 oz) butter
    110 g (4 oz) sugar
    1 teaspoonful baking powder
    110 g (4 oz) currants
    1 egg
    $\frac{1}{4}$ teaspoonful cinnamon

Mix the dry ingredients and rub in the butter. Mix with the egg and roll out the pastry until it is about 1 cm thick.

Use a cardboard shape as a template to make the biscuits in the shape of rabbits or chicks. Bake them in a moderate oven (175 °C, 350 °F or gas mark 4) until they are golden brown.

16. After Easter

The Church's season of Easter continues for six weeks after Easter Day until the eve of Whit Sunday. The Bible says that Jesus appeared to his friends several times between the day of his resurrection and the time when he finally left them. The first occasion was on the road from Jerusalem to a village called Emmaus. Cleopas and his friend were walking along discussing the day's events when Jesus began to walk along with them, although they did not know who their companion was. They repeated to Jesus what had been happening and invited him to spend the night at their house. It was only during supper that they realised who their guest was, whereupon Jesus vanished. The two followers of Jesus returned immediately to Jerusalem to tell the rest of the disciples what had happened.

On the evening of Easter Day the disciples had met in a house and had barred the door because they were afraid that the Jewish authorities might come to arrest them. As they were talking about Jesus' re-appearance, there he was standing among them. They were terrified and thought that they were seeing a ghost. Jesus showed them the wounds in his hands and feet but they were not convinced until he began to eat a piece of fish in front of them. Only then did they realise that this person was in fact Jesus. Thomas was not with them and later refused to believe what the disciples told him. It seemed to him to be a tall story and he said he wouldn't believe it until he saw Jesus for himself. A week later Thomas was with them in a locked room

'Supper at Emmaus'

when Jesus appeared again. This time the disciple believed what he saw but was scolded by Jesus for not believing on the first occasion.

The third time Jesus appeared to the disciples was when seven of them were fishing in the sea of Tiberias. They had spent all night throwing out their nets but by daybreak had caught no fish at all. Then someone advised them from the shore to put out their nets on the starboard side of the boat. They did so and the result was that they caught so many fish that they had to drag their net on to dry land to empty it. John suspected that their strange visitor was Jesus but it was not until they were having their breakfast that they knew for certain. It was on this occasion that Jesus forgave Peter and asked him to take over the leadership of the disciples.

St. John hints in his gospel that Jesus may have appeared at other times to more people, and some scholars have suggested that he may have visited Mary, his mother. The only other incident which is related refers to Jesus 'ascending into heaven'. Jesus and the eleven disciples climbed a hill in the region of Galilee and it was there that he left them for the last time. It is not supposed that the body of Jesus physically rose into the sky.

Christians believe that from that day a new age began when Jesus is present with them wherever they are although they may not be able to see him. The Acts of the Apostles tells the story of the early Christian Church beginning with the new powers which were given to his followers on Whit Sunday.

The Monday, Tuesday and Wednesday before Ascension Day are known as *Rogation* days. The name comes from a Latin word for 'asking' because the purpose of these days is to ask God to bless the crops and fisheries. Some prayers, known as 'litanies', are said on these occasions and a custom is now combined of 'beating the bounds'. This consists of walking round the boundaries of the parish and beating with sticks certain stones or landmarks. Some years ago small boys were also beaten at each of these points to remind them where the parish boundaries were.

Ascension Day is always on a Thursday, exactly forty days after Easter. It is a holy day in most Christian churches and has been observed for the last sixteen hundred years. In some churches the choirs climb to the top of the belfry or tower to sing an Ascension Day hymn. An interesting custom takes place on Ascension Day in Tissington in Derbyshire which was started as far back as AD 1350. As in many places in that county the wells are 'dressed' by being covered with a large picture made up of a mosaic of overlapping flower petals. It is supposed that Tissington's five wells continued to provide water during a severe drought.

Tissington, Derbyshire

There is also a story that, after the Black Death of 1348, the people of Tissington survived the plague because their wells contained pure water. At the Ascension Day ceremony now a service of thanksgiving is held in church followed by a procession to the five wells which are blessed in turn.

Ascension Day is followed nine days later by Whitsun Eve which marks the end of Easter, the season which follows hard on the heels of Twelfth Night and leads into the summer months.

Things to do

1 On an outline map of the Holy Land mark and name the places where Jesus appeared after his resur-

rection. Write a sentence, in a box alongside the place, about each appearance.

2   Read the passages in the gospels which relate the events between Easter and Whitsun Eve.
You will find them in these passages:
  St. Mark: Chapter 16, verses 1 to 8;
  St. John: Chapter 20, verses 1 to 18;
  St. Luke: Chapter 24, verses 13 to 35;
  St. John: Chapter 20, verses 19 to 29;
  St. John: Chapter 21, verses 1 to 17;
  St. Matthew: Chapter 28, verses 16 to 20;
  St. Luke: Chapter 24, verses 50 to 53;
  St. John: Chapter 20, verses 30 and 31.

3   To which people did Jesus appear after his resurrection?
Give the names of the seven disciples and the sons of Zebedee.

4   A person who does not believe what he is told is known as a 'doubting Thomas'.
Make up a story about such a person.

5   A group of children can try to design a religious picture made with flower petals on a slab of clay or plasticine.

6   In the Authorised Version of the Bible it says that it was 'threescore furlongs' from Jerusalem to Emmaus. Work out how far that distance is in our measures.

7   Find out how people caught fish in New Testament times. Draw the fishing boat they used and mark on it the starboard side and the name of the other side of the boat.

8   From a map of the area where you live find the boundaries of your parish, village or town. Beat the bounds and look for any boundary marks or stones.

17. Things to Make for Easter

Easter cards   These are not nearly so popular as Christmas cards but you may like to make a few for your friends or family. Here are some ideas:

A spring flower card can be made by pressing flowers as on page 73. Arrange the flowers on the front of a folded card and glue them carefully into place or cover them with sticky-backed plastic.

An Easter egg card   Fold a piece of strong thick paper or thin card so that the edges overlap slightly.

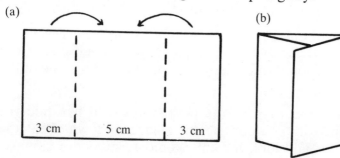

(a)

3 cm   5 cm   3 cm

(b)

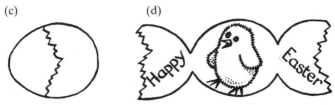

(c)   (d)

Draw and cut out an egg shape on the folded front and make the overlapping edges jagged to represent a cracked egg.

Open the card and inside draw a chick and an Easter greeting.

An Easter chick or bunny card Make a folded card and on the front stick coloured balls of cotton wool to make a chick or bunny. Stick on legs, beaks and eyes made from pieces of gummed paper.

Easter presents

Egg cosies make an unusual Easter gift. You will need 2 yellow pieces of felt 10 cm by 7 cm; scraps of red, white, orange and black felt; glue, needle and cotton.

Place the two pieces of yellow felt together, and round off the top edges.

Out of red felt, cut a comb like this:

and from the orange felt a beak:

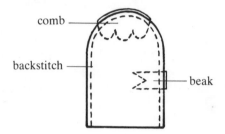

Pin the two pieces of yellow felt together, catching into place the comb and beak, on the inside. Backstitch around the chick, leaving the bottom edge open. Turn the chick inside out and glue on an eye with a circle of white felt, and a black eyeball.

Papier-mâché egg This makes an attractive ornament and is stronger than an ordinary blown egg. You will need an egg, kitchen paper towel or tissues, wallpaper paste, paints and varnish.

Take a blown egg (see page 45) which has been well rinsed and dried. Dip the paper towel or tissue in wallpaper paste and wrap it smoothly around the egg. Repeat this two or three times until you have a smooth surface round the egg. Allow it to dry. Paint a name, face or pattern on the egg and varnish it when dry.

Easter tree In some parts of the United States of America, eggs are hung on to a painted twig to make an Easter tree. Find a twiggy branch and cover it with gold or silver spray or paint. Leave it to dry and then place it in a decorated yoghurt pot or jam jar which has been filled with a stiff mixture of Polyfilla. Glue coloured cotton to the eggs and attach them to the tree. The Easter tree will make an attractive table or room decoration.

Dough basket with eggs This makes a pretty Easter dinner table-decoration but the eggs will be far too hard to eat.

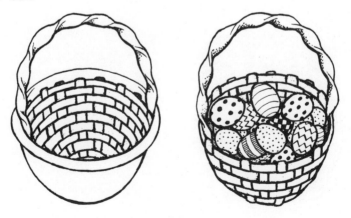

To make the dough you will need 4 cups of plain flour, 1 cup of salt and about $1\frac{1}{2}$ cups of water. Mix the ingredients together until the dough is like pliable, but not too soft, clay.

To make the basket, roll out some dough and cut it into 1 cm wide strips. Line a suitable ovenproof bowl with aluminium foil and then place the strips inside to form a woven effect. Press the joints firmly together. Cut a 2 cm strip to make a handle which should also be pressed firmly in place. To make the eggs take small pieces of dough to form egg shapes. Decorate them by etching patterns on them with a needle or by pressing beads into the dough so that they will be baked in. Put the eggs on an oven tray.

Cook the basket and eggs in the oven at gas mark 3, 325 °F, 160 °C, for $1\frac{1}{2}$ to 2 hours. When they are hard and dry remove them from the oven, slip the basket out of the foil and allow everything to cool. The eggs may now be painted or varnished and piled into the basket. This is best left unpainted as the golden brown colour should give the effect of rushes or osiers. The decoration will keep indefinitely so long as it remains dry.

Reference Material

BBC Radiovision programmes
(for children aged 7 to 10):
'Everything New'
'Spring Awakening'
'Off to the Park'
'Behold, I make all Things New'
'On the Farm'

16 mm colour films:
'Mother Hen's family' (11 minutes)
'Chick, chick, chick' (13 minutes)

These can be hired from Gateway Educational Media, Waverley Road, Yate, Bristol BS17 5RB.

35 mm colour filmstrip:
'Farm animals' (Can be purchased from Gateway Educational Media.)

Books for teachers:
Christina Hole, *Easter and its Customs* (Richard Bell)
Francis X. Weiser, *The Easter Book* (Staples Press)
Christina Hole, *A Dictionary of British Folk Customs* (Paladin, Granada Publishing)
Margaret Baker, *Folklore and Customs of Rural England* (David and Charles Holdings Ltd)
Venetia Newall, *An Egg at Easter: A Folklore Study* (Routledge and Kegan Paul)
Gail Duff, *Country Wisdom* (Pan Books)
J.G. Frazer, *The Golden Bough* (Macmillan Paperback)

Books for children:

What to look for in spring (Ladybird)
Stories of special days and customs (Ladybird)
British wild flowers (Ladybird)
How to make presents (Ladybird)
The Easter story (Ladybird)
Great artists – Book 2 (Ladybird)
Vera Croxford, *Animals in spring* (Transworld Publishers Ltd)
John Simmons, *The life of plants* (Macdonald Educational)
The Noel Streatfield Easter Holiday Book (J.M. Dent)
Colin and Moira Maclean, *A book for spring* (Studio Vista – Cassell & Collier Macmillan Publishers)
Muriel Goaman, *Your book of the year* (Faber & Faber)
Laurence Whistler, *The English Festivals* (Heinemann)
Robin Kerrod, *The Seasons* (Franklin Watts)
Festivals: An anthology compiled by Ruth Manning-Sanders (Heinemann)
G. Ferguson, *Signs and symbols in Christian art* (OUP)
V. Heaton, *The Oberammergau Passion Play* (Hale)
G. Palmer and N. Lloyd, *A year of festivals* (Warne)
D. Waters, *A book of celebrations* (Mills & Boon)

Records and tapes suitable for assemblies:
'Pastoral Symphony' from Handel's Messiah'
'Spring Song' by Mendelsshon
'Spring' from Vivaldi's 'The Four Seasons'
'Spring Symphony' by Benjamin Britten
'On Hearing the First Cuckoo in Spring' by Frederick Delius
'The Cuckoo in the Woods' from 'Carnival of the Animals' by Saint Saens

Musical plays
'The Chicken, the Egg and the Cross' An interpretation of the Easter theme suitable for Junior and Middle Schools. Complete and including stage directions – from Sheila Evans and Ann Palmer, 241 Oldbury Road, St. Johns, Worcester.

'Miracle Man' An Easter musical for Juniors by Kevin Mayhew, 55 Leigh Road, Leigh-on-Sea, Essex SS9 1JP.

'With You Always' and 'No Way Out' By Denis O'Gorman, The Catechetical Centre, 21 Tooting Bec Road, London SW17 8BS.

Anthems and Carols:
'A Spring Cantata' Music by Iain Kendell, words by William Blake and Steuart Allin (J.W. Chester Ltd, 11 Great Marlborough Street, London W1)

'Ring Out, Sing Out' A Festival Carol for Spring by Phyllis Tate (OUP)

'This Joyful Easter-Tide' An anthem for treble voices in two parts, by Dr. G.R. Woodward, arranged by A.E. Baker (A & C Black)

'Lord of the Dance' by Sydney Carter, in *Sing True* (Religious Education Press)

The Oxford Book of Carols Contains an excellent selection of carols for Lent, Passiontide and Easter (OUP)

Someone's Singing Lord Contains spring hymns (A & C Black)

Fifty Songs of Praise and *A Second Fifty Songs of Praise* Contain seasonal and festival carols arranged for recorders. (OUP)

Acknowledgements

The authors and publisher wish to acknowledge the following photograph sources:

BBC Hulton Picture Library   p. 42 (bottom), 55
Jim Brownbill   p. 51
Cadbury Ltd   p. 40
J. Allan Cash   p. 38 (right)
Bruce Coleman/Jane Burton   p. 72
Mary Evans Picture Library   p. 54
Glasgow Art Gallery and Museum   p. 23
The Mansell Collection   p. 9, 17, 21, 30, 57, 59, 63, 64, 65, 80, 84.
The National Gallery   p. 27
Popperfoto   p. 15
The Tate Gallery   p. 66, 67
John Topham Picture Library   p. 3, 7, 32, 38 (left), 42 (top), 47, 71, 86
Zefa   p. 76

The publishers have made every effort to trace the copyright holders, but where they have failed to do so, they will be pleased to make the necessary arrangements at the first opportunity.

Illustrations by Anna Hancock

First published 1984

Published by
MACMILLAN EDUCATION LTD
Companies and representatives
throughout the world

ISBN 0 333 30753 4

Printed in Hong Kong